FIFTY SHADES OF

INSIGHTS THAT BRING LIFE TO
YOUR RELATIONSHIPS

NEW YORK TIMES BEST-SELLING AUTHOR

ED YOUNG

All scripture, unless otherwise noted is the NIV translation –
THE HOLY BIBLE, NEW INTERNATIONAL VERSION®, NIV®
Copyright © 1973, 1978, 1984, 2011 by Biblica, Inc.® Used by
permission. All rights reserved worldwide.
* Excerpt from The Navy SEAL Code
** Jean M. Twenge and W. Keith Campbell, Narcissism Epidemic:
Living in an Age of Entitlement (Atria Books 2010)

Cover Design by Fellowship Church
Cover Illustration by Fellowship Church
Editing by Cara Highsmith, Highsmith Creative Services, www.
highsmithcreative.com

Published in Dallas, Texas by Creality Publishing
Printed in the United States of America
First Edition 14 13 12 11 10 / 10 9 8 7 6 5 4 3 2 1
ISBN 978-1-942306-03-0

This book is dedicated to anyone who wants to get the most out of their relationships. From business partnerships to marriages, classroom acquaintances to lifelong friendships, we all experience relationships. Why? Because life is not a solo sport. We are created as relational beings.

The words, insights, and truths captured on these pages were written to help your relationships grow into a vibrant picture that influences the world around you. Whatever your relational world looks like, this book is in your hands to help you experience another level of meaning and purpose!

TABLE OF
CONTENTS

Preface

PREFACE

I went to high school with a kid named Larry. I'd say we were friends; not close friends, but we hung out a good bit because we played a lot of sports together. After my junior year in high school, my family and I moved from Columbia, South Carolina, all the way to Houston, Texas—1,004 miles away. I pretty much lost contact with Larry until six years later. One night I got a phone call from one of my closest friends.

"Ed," he said, "do you remember Larry?"

I said, "Yes, I remember him."

He said, "Are you sitting down?"

I said, "Yes. Why?"

He said, "Ed, Larry just murdered someone."

I said, "Are you kidding me? Larry?" That was the last thing I expected to hear on the other end of the phone that day. I knew Larry had been getting into some trouble after high school, but murder? What happens in someone's life to take them from being the innocent kid you played basketball with to someone who has been convicted of murder?

Two weeks later I found myself sitting across from Larry at a picnic table in a state penitentiary prison yard. In the midst of our conversation I said, "Larry, I just have to ask you; where did the wheels come off? Where did the problems begin?"

And with tears streaming down his face he responded with four bone-chilling words I will never forget:

"I had these friends . . ."

I had these friends. I can't count how many times I've heard that four-word phrase from people. From junior high school students to high school students, from high school students to college students; from those who are married to those who are single; those with kids and those without; business owners, professional athletes, stay-at-home mothers, and divorced fathers; whenever I talk with someone in the throes of a drug problem or an alcohol abuse situation or violence or anger or illicit behavior or whatever; whenever I ask them, "Where did the wheels come off? When did everything start messing up?" They always start with, "I had these friends . . ."

So often we don't realize the sheer force and influence relationships have in our lives. I would say, generally speaking, the majority of issues we face today all go back to one powerful question: Who are THEY?

For just a moment, take a panoramic look at the relationships in your life. "They" are who you are hanging around, rubbing shoulders with, doing business with, and doing life with. The aspects that shades of color contribute to a work of art—the tiny details that greatly impact the final result—are what "they" mean to your life and mine. It's the undeniable power of "they."

Maybe you recognize the fact that some people in your life are the wrong kind of "they." And, while you may not end up in the penitentiary like my friend Larry, you know they aren't taking you where you need to go. Maybe as you take that panoramic view of those you're closest to, you see some pretty good people. You're pretty sure you're surrounded by the right kind of "they." But how do we know for sure if we're surrounded by the right "they"? This book will unpack fifty simple, sushi-sized servings of truth and insight you can apply to your life to help you find, become, and grow with the right "they."

In my 50-plus years of life, more than thirty years of marriage, more than twenty-five years of ministry, and twenty-eight years of parenting, I've seen all kinds of relationships. I've learned a lot about people. I've seen the relationships of young adults and married couples, families, business partners, and lifelong friends grow, thrive, and leave a lasting legacy. I've also seen the other end of the spectrum with heartbreak and wreckage. What is the difference? They. If you show me who "they" are in your life, I can show you where your life will be in the future.

So, before you turn the page and begin to discover who the right "they" are, what they have, and what they do, I've got to ask you, as you look at your life: Who are "they"?

SHADE ONE:
WHAT IF HE'S RIGHT?

Years ago I was approached by a Hollywood producer to sit down with an adult film actor and discuss our difference in opinions on sexuality. It's not every day you get to sit down and talk openly about the Bible with a porn star, so I thought about it, prayed about it, and obviously talked with my wife Lisa about it. And then, I called this producer and said, "Let's do it, and let's host it here at Fellowship Church."

So, days later, the limousine pulled up, she got out along with her boyfriend/agent who also used to be a porn star, and we sat down, cameras rolling, to begin the discussion.

Her argument out of the gate was, "I help marriages. I help spice up their sex life," she said. "I help give singles a sexual release. I like to live on the edge, and it's not like I'm hurting anyone."

We talked for some time. I answered many of her questions about God and the Bible. Then, after a while I said, "Think about sex as you would a Maserati. What if you gave me a Maserati? I would take excellent care of the car. I wouldn't take it off-roading. I wouldn't trash it or mess it up." Then I said, "You might not realize it, but you are taking this Maserati—sex—and going off-roading with it. You are taking the content (sex) out of the right context (marriage), and it's only going to lead to chaos. I've counseled enough people and seen enough lives damaged and destroyed by pornography to know it's not going to work for you."

I went on to say, "Do you know why you are here? It's not for a television show. You're here because God has driven you here. You are young and you have your whole life ahead of you, and if you truly want to live on the edge, if you want the best, if you want to discover how good God is, you have to give it all to Him."

She began to lean in and got teary-eyed. You could see the gears turning in her head. Obviously God had orchestrated our paths for a purpose greater than what that Hollywood producer had. And as she left the church that day she turned to her boyfriend and said, "What if he's right?"

One day, Jesus had an encounter with a woman who wasn't much different from the girl I spoke with that day (John 4). Jesus didn't judge the woman for her past. He didn't ridicule her for who she chose to surround herself with. He simply offered her something better in life. And her response was the same as this girl I spoke with. In essence she asked, "What if he's right?"

That four-word question reveals a powerful truth. Too often, we can be surrounded by people who only give us one perspective on life. The girl I spoke with was a card-carrying example of what it looks like to be surrounded by the wrong "they" and to be led astray. But she's not alone.

As you read this, no matter what age and stage of life you're in, no matter what shade of relationship you're dealing with, my belief is this book didn't cross your path by coincidence. There's something better out there for you. And my prayer is that you will ask the same question that girl asked that day: "What if he's right?"

The righteous choose their friends carefully. . . .
—Proverbs 12:26

SHADE TWO:
RELATIONAL NOUN

Everyone—from porn stars to teachers, convicted felons to housewives, young professionals to professional athletes—has to ask the question, "What if he's right?"

Does it really matter where we go? Does it matter who we hang out with? The answer is yes. It's all about relational nouns—people, places, and things. Because, if we hang around the wrong people, we'll end up going to the wrong places, and we'll wind up doing the wrong things.

Perhaps your past isn't written exactly as my friend's who sat across the picnic table from me in the prison yard. Likely, your past isn't written in the same way as that porn star I met. But could it be that your past reflects the story of the biblical character Samson?

The Cliff's Notes© of Samson's life are tragic. He went from having everything going for him—incredible strength, purpose, blessed by God—to someone shacked up with a high-class call girl who betrayed him with a haircut in Satan's Salon. With the loss of his hair, he lost his strength, was seized, had his eyes gouged out, was imprisoned, and eventually died. Where did it all go wrong?

Samson went down to Timnah.
—Judges 14:1

Timnah was a place Samson knew he should not have gone. A place built on sex and seduction—the worst place for a he-man with a she-weakness to be.

Samson hooked up with the wrong people, the Philistines. These people didn't believe in God. They didn't honor God. They didn't have Samson's best in mind. And the dominoes of compromise began to fall, taking him further and further away from God's purpose for his life. I'm sure he thought, *Just this once I'll go down to Timnah.* But "just this once" always leads to another "just this once."

So often what you chase in your attempt to experience freedom often ends up enslaving you! That's what happened to Samson. How different would his story have been had he not gone down to Timnah? What if he hadn't surrounded himself with the wrong people?

Are the "they" in your life leading you down the path of "just this once," down the path to Timnahtation? (Temptation in case you missed that.) Maybe your past reflects Samson's story, but your future doesn't have to! Link up with the right "they" who will protect your purpose. When you surround yourself with the right people, you'll wind up going to the right places, and you'll end up doing the things that will help you reach your full potential!

SHADE THREE:
TOUGH

In Samson's life, we see the wrong "they" reflected in who he hung out with, where he went, and what he ended up doing. But the right "they" are just the opposite. We find them in the right places and they inspire and challenge us to do the right things. But who are the right they?

The right "they" are:

Tough
Honest
Encouraging
Yielded

I had the opportunity recently to interview Marcus Luttrell, retired Navy SEAL and author of the book *Lone Survivor*. Marcus has a remarkable story of putting his life on the line not only for his country, but also the men he fought alongside. During our conversation, he gave me insight into this by sharing a portion of the Navy SEAL Code* with me:

I will never quit. I persevere and thrive on adversity. My Nation expects me to be physically harder and mentally stronger than my enemies. If knocked down, I will get back up, every time. I will draw on every remaining ounce of strength to protect my teammates and to accomplish our mission. I am never out of the fight.

The right THEY are never out of the fight. We may not have a Navy SEAL in our corner all the time, but when a moment in life comes that knocks us to our knees, we need people who will stand with us, fight for us, strengthen us, and emerge with us on the other side. We can't win this fight on our own.

In my own life, the right "they" have strengthened me time and time again. Over the course of my life, and specifically my ministry, there have been so many times I've wanted to throw in the towel. When we first began Fellowship Church over twenty-five years ago things were very difficult. One time in particular, just a few months in, I had had enough. I remember coming home and telling Lisa, "I quit. I don't want to do this anymore. I think maybe God has something else for us."

And I'll never forget what she said: "This is what we've prayed for. This is where God has brought us. We have a purpose here. God wants to use us."

It was exactly what I needed to hear. I knew in my heart of hearts that she was right. I just needed someone tough enough to remind me that the fight we were in was worth the effort. Lisa and several others have been the tough voices over the years that have strengthened me in those moments of doubt to help me stay in the fight. Not only did they strengthen me with their words to hang on, they were willing to stand with me and fight. And because of that, we've been able to emerge from fight after fight toward the purpose God has for our lives.

SHADE FOUR:
HONEST

The right "they" are:

Tough
Honest
Encouraging
Yielded

Have you ever heard the phrase, "*To be honest with you . . .*"? Does that statement ever raise suspicion in you like it does me?

It's a colloquialism that a lot of people use. I'm sure some say this out of habit or as an introductory phrase that seems harmless, but hearing these words does bring us to an important question: does that mean everything else they've said isn't honest?

The right "they" are honest, real, and truthful.

Whenever you have someone who likes to exaggerate, watch out. Whenever you have someone who always has to one-up your story, watch out. If someone who's married says, "Don't tell my spouse . . . ," or if a coworker whispers to you, "Let's keep this between us so the boss doesn't find out;" or students, if your friends say, "Don't tell your parents . . . ," then let me say it again: watch out!

Whether bold lies, exaggerations, little white lies, half-truths, cover-ups, or deception—they all lead down the wrong path. Steer clear of liars. You need to be surrounded by people you can trust, and you cannot trust someone who is not always honest.

The right "they" tell the truth, the whole truth, and nothing but the truth!

Do not lie to each other, since you have taken off your old self with its practices and have put on the new self, which is being renewed in knowledge in the image of its Creator.
—Colossians 3:9-10

SHADE FIVE:
ENCOURAGING

The right "they" are:

Tough
Honest
Encouraging
Yielded

Life is too short to be surrounded by doggie downers. It's too precious to be surrounded by people who drench your dreams with cold water or muddle your mind with doubt. I want to go where I'm celebrated, not just where I'm tolerated! Life is challenging enough as it is without having to be discouraged by those closest to you.

The right "they" are encouraging.

There's a great story in the Bible that exemplifies this shade. Shadrach, Meshach, and Abednego were three friends (Jews) who were living in exile in Babylon, thousands of miles away from their home. And the king in the territory, King Nebuchadnezzar, set an edict that everyone must bow down to a golden statue of himself when the trumpets sounded. But these three friends refused to bow to anyone or anything other than God. And as a result, they were thrown into a fire.

Don't you know these guys were dealing with some serious fear? Don't you know they faced some serious thoughts of bailing? Yet, they encouraged one another so they could withstand the literal fires of adversity they faced. You know these guys had to encourage one another to get through the ordeal!

How do you feel after spending time with the people in your life? Are you encouraged? Or do you feel depleted and negative? If so, you're in a releechionship, not a relationship. A releechionship is a relationship that sucks the life out of you and replaces your dreams with doubts and your enthusiasm with skepticism.

Several years ago I was wading through a

swamp with a friend of mine named Biff from west Texas. Biff was a Marine who served in Vietnam. After we got back to Biff's car, I was taking my shoes and socks off and noticed a giant, black, leaf-looking thing on my calf. I tried to brush it off, but it wouldn't budge. Then it began to move.

Biff looked over at me and said, "Huh. Ed, you got a big ol' leech on you, man. We used to have those in the jungles of Vietnam. You know what we have to do, right? We just have to burn it off!" And that's exactly what he did.

The right "they" know what it takes to burn off those leeches: encouragement!

Get rid of the releechionships in your life! Stick with those who energize you, who fuel you, who love you for who you are, and who help you move forward in life.

Let us consider how we may spur one another on toward love and good deeds.
—Hebrews 10:24

SHADE SIX:
YIELDED

The right "they" are:

Tough
Honest
Encouraging
Yielded

Isn't it awesome to have people who say yes without hesitation or need for an explanation when we ask for something? It's refreshing. It's not about them cowering or caving in just to shut us up. It's about saying yes with understanding and trust.

We need to surround ourselves with Yes-men and Yes-women. But they don't just say yes to us, they say yes to God.

If I had to choose one aspect of the right "they"

as the most important, this one would be it. This is the foundation that every other shade builds itself on.

Look at the word they. What do you see right in the middle? HE! The right they have God in the center of their lives! They have said yes to God and have yielded to him in every area of their lives.

When you have a person who at the end of the day arrives consistently at the conclusion that God is God and they are not, and they yield to him, you have a person God is going to be able to do some amazing things in and through.

Think about a yield sign you would see on the road. What does it look like? It looks like someone who is standing with their arms raised to God! The right "they" are yielded to God!

Trust in the Lord with all your heart and lean not on your own understanding; in all your ways submit to him, and he will make your paths straight.
—Proverbs 3:5-6

SHADE SEVEN:
THE POWER OF THE TONGUE

"They said . . . "

"They've been coming to me . . ."

"They told me . . . "

"They do . . ."

"They don't . . ."

"They . . ."

"They" always have something to say, don't they?

When our kids were younger, we took a vacation with several friends. One night after a big meal, all of the children started doing these cool things with their bodies. They made a contest of summersaults, push-ups, cartwheels, and other odd contortions. They were trying to show off for all of the parents.

After a while they asked us, "Hey, Mom and Dad, can you guys do anything cool with your bodies?" Not to shy away from a challenge, my wife, Lisa, can do this really wild thing. She can throw her hip out of joint. So she did that, and the kids were thinking, "Whoa, a double-jointed Mom! Pretty wild!"

Then the competition shifted to funny faces and tricks with their tongues. They were making all kinds of crazy shapes with their tongues. Then they asked me, "Dad, can you do this?" (and they rolled their tongues). I couldn't do it. I still can't do it. For some reason, I just can't roll my tongue. You know that piece of skin on the bottom of your tongue that holds it down? Mine is really big, and it keeps me from rolling my tongue. I call it my tongue tamer.

When it comes to the words we speak, we all need that tongue tamer, don't we? The right "they" know that the power of the tongue is monumental.

Our tongues have the power to build others up or to tear them down. We can either speak life or death into someone's life. We can go negative on people and spit and spew our negativity on people. If we aren't careful, we can speak death over someone. Or, like the right "they," we can learn to speak life.

Speaking life is as easy as encouraging someone when they are facing a tough situation. It's giving your spouse a compliment. It's telling your children that you love them and are proud of them.

You've heard the saying, "If you don't have anything nice to say, don't say anything at all." What that is really saying is, "Don't speak death into people's lives; speak life!"

The tongue has the power of life and death, and those who love it will eat its fruit.
—Proverbs 18:21

The right "they" know the power of the tongue. And they use it to help build others up rather than tear them down.

SHADE EIGHT: GRACE AND CONSEQUENCES

The right "they" use their words to build others up rather than tear them down. They also use their words to wake others up rather than watch them drown. When you have the right "they" in your life, you have people who can help you stay on God's path for your life—the ultimate path.

One of the most scandalous stories on relationships is found in the Bible. The leading characters are a man named David, a woman named Bathsheba, and another man named Nathan.

David was a king known for being a man after God's own heart. One day, he stood on the roof of his palace walking along the edge and the ledge where he caught a glimpse of a beautiful woman named Bathsheba who was bathing on the roof below. David knew she was married, but her beauty overthrew his good judgment and he sent for her, and they slept together.

Now, if this were a movie, the storyline could very easily end here. The picture our culture and media paint of sex and relationships is such an illusion. They present to us the idea of a world where there are little, if any, consequences for our actions. The upside of sin is enjoyed so often without the downside of the consequences being shown. But the reality is that there are consequences for every choice we make. Had David consulted Nathan—the right "they"—he would have avoided the wrong turn he made.

The plot clots when Bathsheba becomes pregnant. David could not have this on his resume, so he crafted a plan to have her husband killed in battle. David thought his cleverness had covered his tracks. The baby came and he was in the clear. But the story didn't end there. Eventually God exposed what he had done, and David had to face some serious consequences.

The right "they" help us stay far away from the edge and ledge of compromise and sin. They help us see ahead to the consequences of our actions. God used Nathan (David's right "they") in a big way in this story. Nathan didn't sweep David's choices under the rug. He didn't turn the other way and let David continue down the path of wrong choices. Instead, he confronted David with the truth, in love.

Now, the beauty of this story is that, in the end, David hit his knees in prayer, came clean, and sought forgiveness from God. Ultimately, God forgave him and continued to write an amazing story with David's life. Why? Because God cares more about our next step than our misstep.

God is a God of grace, but that doesn't mean there will not be consequences in our lives for the decisions we make. If I rob a bank, I'll get arrested. Now, if I hit my knees on the jailhouse floor and ask God to forgive me, will he? Absolutely. But will I still be in jail? YES!

If a person has sex before marriage, or is looking at pornography, or is cheating on their spouse, will God forgive them if they seek his forgiveness? Without question. Will there be some complications that arise in their life? Without question. God's forgiveness of our actions doesn't negate the consequences we face.

So when it comes to the choices you make in your relationships, ask yourself, "How could this play out?" And stay away from the edge and ledge of compromise.

SHADE NINE:
FENCES

How do you stay away from the edge and ledge of compromise? Boundaries.

My wife Lisa and I love dogs. We've had everything from maltipoos and English mastiffs to dachshunds and Doberman pinschers. So what do you expect to find in our yard? Fences. These fences serve two tremendous purposes: they are there to protect our dogs, and they are there to protect others.

We can learn from David's mistakes by putting up fences in our lives that protect our relationships and keep us from walking near the edge and ledge of compromise.

> *The highway of the upright avoids evil; those who guard their ways preserve their lives.*
> —Proverbs 16:17

Here are a few "fences" Lisa and I have put in our lives to protect our marriage:

1. We do not have meals with or ride in a car alone with a member of the opposite sex. When we need to meet with a member of the opposite sex, we either include a third party or leave the door open where our meeting can be audible and visible to anyone around.

2. We do not share details about our marriage with a member of the opposite sex. The intimate details of our relationship are just that: intimate. They are for us and us alone. Marriage is sacred. No one outside of the marriage needs to hear those sacred, intimate details.

3. We do not share emotion with members of the opposite sex in person or via technology. In fact, we hardly communicate with members of the

opposite sex through technology period. Technology (email, texts, social media, etc.) are tools for communicating logistics rather than emotion.

Here is a list of fences we would recommend for those who are in a dating relationship in order to protect their relationships and future marriages:

1. Avoid hanging out one-on-one with a member of the opposite sex in an environment where you have zero accountability. In other words, don't put yourself in a position that could cause you to compromise.

2. Don't spend all of your time with the person you date. You need to get a well-rounded picture of this person, and that takes input from other right "they" people in your life. Make sure you are spending time with others who can help you get a full picture of who you are dating.

3. Do not live together. Period. Don't buy into the lie that this will give you a taste of what marriage is like. Rather, see the truth that it will likely ruin whatever chance you have for your marriage being a success.

God puts fences up to protect us and to protect others. The right "they" understand that fact and are excellent helpers in building those fences!

SHADE TEN:
CONTROL

Not only do we need fences in our relationships with others, but we need fences for ourselves behind closed doors as well.

A popular theme in the world of sex these days is control. Men and women fight over control of the checkbook, control of the remote, and control in the bedroom. I am all for control; however, not control over one another but control over our personal thoughts and desires. The Bible tells us to,

> *Take captive every thought and make it obedient to Christ.*
> —2 Corinthians 10:5

What's your sexual strategy? What boundaries are you setting up for yourself to help you control your thoughts? Do you have a game plan to avoid temptation and sin?

Now, let me be clear. Temptation is not sin, but it is usually the step that leads to sin. What is sin? Sin is simply an archery term that means "to miss the mark." Temptation can get us to miss the mark—the bull's-eye—of God's best for our lives. Certain temptations cannot be avoided. However, if we have a game plan and set up intentional boundaries, we can avoid a lot of the temptation and hit the bull's-eye more often.

- Geographical control: Where are the places you should avoid going? Where do you go that causes you to be at your weakest?
- Emotional control: What revs your emotional engines and makes you vulnerable to poor choices?
- Technology and Media control: What TV channels or websites do you need to cancel or put a filter on?
- Physical control: What are things you need to physically do to avoid falling into sin?

Here's a quick example of how this played out in my life once. One day, Lisa and I were sitting on the beach at a beautiful resort. A friend of ours, who was with us, saw some people she wanted to introduce to us, so she called out to them to come over. I looked up and saw a beautiful woman coming our way. I've seen more cotton in an aspirin bottle than what this woman was wearing!

Now, I had a pair of sunglasses on that completely hid my eyes, so even though Lisa was sitting right beside me, there is no way she could see what I was looking at. I had a choice to make. I could leave my sunglasses on, which would allow me to look anywhere I wanted without anyone seeing my eyes. Or I could take the sunglasses off, making it very difficult for my eyes (and thus my mind) to go where they should not.

It's situations like this one where we need to learn to control our thoughts. I'm not perfect, but in that situation, I took my sunglasses off— exposing my eyes and keeping myself from missing the bull's-eye that God has for my life.

"I have the right to do anything," you say—but not everything is beneficial. "I have the right to do anything"—but I will not be mastered by anything.
—1 Corinthians 6:12

When it comes to controlling our thoughts, there are some very practical things that we can do. Guys, I heard Billy Graham say years ago that it's not the first look that gets you into trouble; it's the second and third looks that do. So don't take those second glances. Keep your eyes up.

Ladies, I've heard that those envy engines can get revved up in your lives from time to time. In situations where you are beginning to feel a twinge of jealousy, say a quick prayer of thanks for something in your life. Choose to focus on what you have rather than what you don't have.

The right "they" know how to control their thoughts because they know who is in control of their lives—and that's God. The moment we give up control to him is the moment we gain control.

SHADE ELEVEN:
FEELINGS ARE FREAKY

Confession: I don't always feel like giving God control. I don't always feel like working. I don't always feel like loving my wife, Lisa, or our four kids. I didn't feel like writing this page. I don't *feel* like doing a lot of things.

A problem with our world today is that everything is feelings-based. You don't feel like working on your marriage? Quit. You don't feel like telling this person the truth? Don't. Go with your feelings. The problem with that is that feelings are freaky. My feelings are subject to physical, emotional, and spiritual drain.

Now let me be clear. Feelings aren't always bad. God has feelings. He wants us to feel as well. But the danger comes when we live our lives based on those feelings because feelings are freaky.

You've heard the expression "Listen to your

heart," but have you ever heard this?

The heart is deceitful above all things and beyond cure. Who can understand it?

—Jeremiah 17:9

That's not a verse likely to make the side of a coffee mug. Maybe I'm feeling a certain way because I ate some bad sushi. Maybe I am overdramatizing a situation in my mind. Or maybe I'm just tired.

How can you make sure you aren't living based on your feelings? You've got to HALT! Never make decisions that matter when you are too Hungry, Angry, Lonely, or Tired. Don't make important decisions on an empty stomach, in the heat of emotion, in the midst of isolation, or at the point of exhaustion because, in those moments, you won't feel like doing the right thing. If you wait to feel like doing what you're supposed to do, there are many times you would never do it. You may just be too hungry. Maybe you need to take a walk and calm down. Maybe you need a good friend to listen in that moment. Or maybe you just need a nap!

Whatever it is, the right "they" don't try to feel their way into an action. Instead, they act their way into a feeling. Commitments take feeling out of the mix of the decision-making. The right "they" don't live based on feelings. They are people we can bounce our feelings off of because they understand that sometimes you have to act your way into a feeling.

SHADE TWELVE: UNLEASHING UNFORGIVENESS

Speaking of feelings, have you ever felt like forgiving someone who has wronged you? NO! And neither have I.

I'll never forget this scene, which perfectly illustrates what I mean. I was filling up my car at a gas station when this guy walked up with his Doberman Pinscher and leashed it up to a bench that was anchored in concrete outside the store, and then he walked inside to get a drink.

All of a sudden, something startled the dog. You could see the whites of his eyes. Then, in a flash, he took off on a mad dash toward the busy freeway. He took off with such force—with such torque—that he ripped the bench out of its supports, right out of the cement! He dragged this thing behind him, sparks flew, and I thought this dog was going to get hit by a car!

But, as he tore off into the intersection, cars, trucks, and SUVs screeched to a stop. And this dog, still leashed to the bench, stopped short of one vehicle and changed direction on a dime. The bench he was dragging, though, didn't have his reaction time. It kept heading in the same direction, until it slammed into the side of an SUV. Bam! Then, as the dog ran in the other direction, the bench went barreling behind him. Bam! The bench slammed into another car. Parts were flying everywhere! I just stood there in complete shock.

When it comes to relationships, how many people are like that Doberman? They are making their way through life, leashed up and tied up to a bench—a bench of unforgiveness.

Maybe you've been hurt in the past. Maybe someone betrayed you. Maybe the person who hurt you is dead! Who is sitting on your bench? While you don't realize it, you are dragging this bench around through life and it's causing some serious collateral damage in your relationships. It's damaging your life and other's lives.

The right "they" don't stay leashed up to

unforgiveness, and we shouldn't either. Don't allow a past hurt to damage your life today or your potential tomorrow. Instead, unleash unforgiveness, release this person to God, and begin living your life without carrying all that weight behind.

Then Peter came to Jesus and asked, "Lord, how many times shall I forgive my brother or sister who sins against me? Up to seven times?" Jesus answered, "I tell you, not seven times, but seventy-seven times."

—Matthew 18:21-22

SHADE THIRTEEN: MASTERING THE MASERATI

At the beginning of this book I used a Maserati as an illustration for sex, stating that if you were given a Maserati, you wouldn't take it off-roading; would you? Not unless you'd lost your mind! No. A Maserati is designed to be driven on the open road.

The same way a Maserati is not designed to drive off-road, we were not designed to have sex outside the context of marriage. God designed sex and we're designed to have a lot of it, but within the guidelines and guardrails of marriage.

The right "they" drive in the right gears at the right time.

Prior to marriage, they keep it in first gear, the cuddling gear. This is the gear that allows you to keep a good read on the car you are driving. You aren't going too fast, and you aren't in danger of skidding out of control. It's the time when you warm up to each other and get to know one another. It's crucial to stay in this gear while you are dating. Why? Because, once you shift on up to second gear, the caressing gear, the engines really start revving. Things are getting heated, and it's difficult to shift back down. The Maserati at this point is ready to move to top speed. If we shift up to this second gear before marriage, it will easily lead us into third gear, the climax gear.

Second and third gears are designed to be used on the autobahn of marriage. Otherwise, we aren't using the car the way it was designed by the Designer. It's like driving with the windows fogged up; you can't even get a good read on your surroundings. You can't tell if you are cruising around with the right "they" in your driver's seat or not, and you pick up so much speed that you lose control of the car and end up in the ditch with a damaged and wrecked Maserati.

Flee from sexual immorality. All other sins a person commits are outside the body, but whoever sins sexually, sins against their own body.

—1 Corinthians 6:18

Don't try to master the Maserati on your own. Keep sex sexy. And give your Maserati to the Master.

SHADE FOURTEEN: WHO'S IN THE DRIVER'S SEAT?

Speaking of Maseratis, maybe I'm the only one, but anytime I see an amazingly unique car cruising around, such as a Maserati, I can't help but try to sneak a glance to see if I can recognize the person driving it. Surely I'm not the only one who does that. I want to know who's in the driver's seat!

There are a lot of great qualities to look for in a person. But the ultimate thing we should be looking for is who or what is in the driver's seat of that person's life? In other words, do they rely on their relationship with God? Or are they trying to do it all themselves?

The Bible says in 2 Corinthians 6:14,

Do not be yoked together with unbelievers.

Maybe you're thinking, "Man, Ed, that's harsh. I thought the Bible was a book about love and peace." That's exactly what is driving this verse: love so you can experience peace.

Imagine my wife Lisa and I were trying to fix an issue on a car, but I was reading the owner's manual to a Ford F-150 and she was reading the owner's manual to a Rolls Royce. There would be major issues that we wouldn't be able to resolve! We'd be trying to solve a problem using two completely different manuals and philosophies.

Sadly, I've seen marriage after marriage crash and burn because they failed to check and see who was in the driver's seat before they walked down the wedding runner.

God is the designer of our lives. He knows the best way we should function and what it takes for us to reach our full potential. The right "they" have handed over the keys of their lives to Jesus and are allowing him to sit in the driver's seat.

SHADE FIFTEEN: THE THREE "YOU" TYPES

When you ask the question, "Who are they?" you'll find that there are three answers you can have. Because when it comes to the "they" in your life, you'll find three different types of people: "For You," "Use You," and "With You" types.

To know who you have in your life, do a friendventory and ask yourself which one of these categories they fall into.

- "For You" people are your fans. They're cheering you on from the sidelines when things are going great and booing you from the cheap seats the second conflict stirs up. The "for you" type changes loyalties like a chameleon changes colors.

- "Use You" people get close for their own personal gain. They will give just enough to get what they need from you. Do you wonder if someone is a "use you" person? Ask yourself, "Do they have a desperate need to be needed? Are they continually climbing?" If so, they'll just end up using you as another rung on the ladder.

- "With You" people are the real deal. These are the right "they." These people are diamonds, not decoys. How do you know if they are a "With You" person? When you go through conflict, turn around and see who still has your back. Those are the right "they."

"With you" people don't need an explanation from you; "use you" and "for you" types won't believe one if you gave it to them.

In a world that says, "It's all about how many friends and followers you have," I would encourage you to focus on the "With You" people. Too often, the followers in our lives should actually be called "hollowers," because that's how loyal most of them are.

In the Old Testament, King David surrounded himself with the right "they." These were people who had proven themselves on the battlefield. They had walked through the fires of attacks. They stayed strong and continued to prove themselves over and over again. And the only question David ever asked them was, "Are you with me?" David knew that "with you" people are the only people to do life and battle with.

Are the people in your life with you? The right "they" will be.

SHADE SIXTEEN:
CRAZY PILL

I left out a category of people to look out for during your friendventory: crazy people!

Do you ever look around and wonder, "Am I the only person who hasn't taken my crazy pills?" Our world is going crazy. It's crazy on the freeways. The economy is crazy. The housing market? Crazy. Relationships? Crazy. Terrorism? Crazy. The government? Well . . . our world is going crazy. We just live in crazy world. Everything is CRAZY.

But if the truth were known, all of us have a cup of crazy in our family recipe. Like the famous Ozzy Osbourne song, we can all end up on a crazy train! We all have an element of craziness. But it's not all bad. There's normal crazy and then there's crazy-crazy.

I say "normal crazy" in jest because each of us, with our sin nature, demonstrates that, without

God, we have a form of craziness. God, though, brings sanity to our lives through Christ. And the more we walk with God and yield to his truth, the further away from that craziness we get. That's normal crazy we all deal with.

But the question that begs to be answered is this: In our search for the right "they," how do we know if we're dealing with a crazy-crazy person? How do you know if you're dealing with somebody who swallowed a crazy pill?

We need discernment to know which is which. Discernment is simply the ability to separate one option from another, one decision from another. So how do you know if you're dealing with someone who swallowed the crazy pill? What can help you discern the truth? Ten things . . .

1. They have crazy eyes. You've seen that person with a weird stare or who shows the whites of their eyes at all times. They're locked in on extreme emotion constantly.
2. They always play the "God" card. To them, the statement, "Well, God told me . . ." means they have a license to do whatever they want to do.

3. They are a name-dropper.
4. They are a one-upper. They'll one up you on EVERYTHING. You went to the lake for the weekend; they spent a week at an exclusive beach resort.
5. They blow up your phone, email, and text relentlessly.
6. They ask for advice, but rarely take it. They enjoy their dysfunction and don't really want to change or improve.
7. They always talk about themselves. "I, I, I, me, me, me, my, my, my." Every question they ask you is really just a set up for them to talk about themselves.
8. They don't have a filter. "I just say what's on my mind. I'm just keeping it real. I don't mean to offend you, but . . ."
9. They usually lock onto one issue and simply won't let it go.
10. They are space invaders. They love to get up in your personal space.

If you find you are marking yes by all of these, then you know you're dealing with a crazy-crazy, and not the right "they." Stay away, because crazy-

crazy people will monopolize your time and keep you away from the right "they"!

SHADE SEVENTEEN: SECRETS

Do you want to sign yourself up for a ride on that crazy train? One surefire way to do it is to stow away some secrets!

When our twins were three years old I took them fishing at a little lake near our house. We had a great time, and we caught a bunch of perch. They were having a blast, shouting, "Oh, Dad, look at this perch!"

As we caught them, I told them, "Girls, we practice catch and release. So when you catch a fish, throw it back. We're not going to keep them. Throw them back."

After about an hour, we started to pack everything up and head back to the house. I got my tackle box, threw my rods and reels in the truck, and drove home. When we got home, we put everything up in the garage where we kept all the fishing gear.

Wind the clock forward three days—three days of triple-digit Texas heat—and we began to smell something in the house. It was the worst odor you could ever experience! But we couldn't find the source of it. We searched everywhere—under carpets, behind doors, in boxes. None of us could figure out what it was.

Then, something told me I needed to go back and check the fishing gear. So I went to the garage and opened up the tackle box I had put away three days before. When I opened it, I found a dead fish! One of the twins, behind my back, had put a fish in my tackle box rather than releasing it back into the water. Three days of dead, rotting, stinking fish hit me all at once, and the smell about bowled me over!

Secrets in a relationship are a lot like that fish. Too often we hide them from the ones we love, thinking we can keep them concealed. But eventually the stench leaks out and the discovery can be catastrophic.

The Bible says, *Whoever conceals their sins does not prosper, but the one who confesses and renounces them finds mercy.*

—Proverbs 28:13

In other words, what we cover God will uncover, but what we uncover God will cover. What we uncover, God will cover in his grace and mercy.

Remember, you are only as sick as your secrets. The enemy will lie to you and convince you, "If you share this secret, they'll judge you. They won't love you. Just hide it. Things will be better."

But just the opposite is true! When we share our secrets, reveal our feelings with the right "they" in our lives, they'll tell us, "I deal with the same thing!" The empathy and healing will be amazing. The right "they" understand that the revealing of your feelings is the beginning of healing!

There is value in vulnerability and insanity in isolation. We need the right "they" in our lives who we can confess our secrets to, who challenge us to uncover them, and who stick by our side as we journey through the steps that follow.

SHADE EIGHTEEN:
BRIDGING THE GAP

Before we jump off the crazy train, I want to hit two final, major topics. When you read these two words, at first you won't think they're crazy. But just stick with me for the next few minutes while you read. What am I talking about? Priorities and commitments.

Crazy, right? Well, maybe not yet. But stay with me here.

Priorities are the things we say are most important. Commitments are the things we do to carry out those commitments. It sounds simple enough, right? After all, if we say it's important, surely we will do what we need to in order to follow up on it.

Well, years ago I read an article in the Harvard

Business Review that revealed a study of Americans in today's fast-paced, over-committed world. And the results were astonishing. It stated that our priorities aren't the problem. Most people say they have the same priorities. The gap, the delta, the chasm comes with commitments. Harvard concluded that many people are committed, but they're committed to the wrong things and most of our commitments don't line up with our priorities.

No wonder so many of our lives feel crazy and chaotic! Our commitments have slowly and discreetly led us away from our priorities.

The right "they" have priorities that are underscored by their commitments.

The Bible teaches us that our priorities should be listed in this order: God, spouse, family, career. So goes my relationship with God, so goes my marriage. So goes my marriage, so goes our family. So goes our family, so goes my career, and so on.

Great businesses, great restaurants, and great marriages all have one thing in common: they keep the main thing the main thing. They have their priorities in line, and they follow those priorities up with the commitments they make.

The right "they" in your life are the same. They don't get caught up in the superfluous; they focus on the significant.

So often, good is the enemy of great. There are a lot of good things in life that we can say yes to, but if we aren't careful, all those good things will cause us to miss out on the great things. We can end up committing to the wrong things. So, how do we bridge the gap? By making sure our commitments match our priorities.

Lisa and I have made it a priority to put our marriage above our careers, even above our children, and so we go on a weekly date night. That's a tangible, real-time way for us to keep our marriage at the top of our list of priorities. Now, inevitably, there are opportunities that present themselves all the time on this night, but we continue to say no to those good things so we can say yes to our marriage. It's so easy to say yes to this commitment, yes to that commitment, and before we know it, our priorities are nothing but a list of ideals.

The right "they" follow up what they say with what they do. What in your life do you need to start saying no to so you can say yes to the best?

SHADE NINETEEN: WHO AM I?

Finding the right "they" in life is important. But equally important is becoming the right "they." To have a friend you have to be a friend. And the kind of friend you are is the kind of friend you will attract. It's a two-way street.

The Bible says,

Two are better than one, because they have a good return for their labor: If they fall down, they can help each other up. But pity those who fall and have no one to help them up.
—Ecclesiastes 4:9-10

Life is not a solo sport. We are all created to be relational beings. We need those healthy relationships in life, and we need to be those healthy relationships for others.

Are you someone people know they can count on? Are you . . .

- Tough – Will you stand strong in the midst of your friends' difficulties?
- Honest – Do you speak the truth in love to people in a way that builds them up?
- Encouraging – Do you celebrate your friends' successes and encourage them beyond any failure?
- Yielded – Have you put God as the number one priority in your life and yielded everything to him?

As you continue reading these fifty shades, don't just think about the "they" in your life; think about yourself as well. You could very well be the right "they" someone needs in their life.

SHADE TWENTY: MAN'S BEST FRIEND

I mentioned this earlier, but Lisa and I love dogs. We have had so many throughout the years—you name it, we've probably had it.

We've learned a lot from our dogs; so, who better to take advice from when it comes to the right "they" than from man's best friend?

Here's a list handed down from our dogs that I like to call the K-9-ments:

1. The right "they" are fiercely loyal.
2. The right "they" shake it off. They can shake off our shortcomings because they know that we are all in need of grace.
3. The right "they" know their name and who they are in God's eyes.
4. The right "they" bark when something's wrong—they speak up.
5. The right "they" sniff it out. They have great

discernment and can tell when something doesn't smell right.

6. The right "they" know attitude is important. They don't bring us down with negativity, but rather they enjoy life and our company.

7. The right "they" like to nap. They honor God by resting from their work, going to church, and giving God the first day of their week.

8. The right "they" obey their master. Jesus said in John 14:15 (NLT), "If you love me, obey my commands."

9. The right "they" know a little praise goes a long way. They know the power of their words and they use theirs to praise you!

I'm sorry, but I've never learned anything useful from cats!

SHADE TWENTY-ONE: "THEY" INSPECTION

I will never forget what happened when Lisa and I bought our first home. We found a little place that we fell in love with. Before we went to the mortgage company and put our money down, we paid for an inspection. Since we were buying the house directly from the owner, we accompanied the inspector to the house. We wanted to watch him check out the entire place.

When we walked in the front door, we saw the owners sitting on the hearth in the family room. I thought that was little odd, but I decided that they were just being nice and giving us operating room to look around and see that everything was okay.

Over the next hour or so, the inspector looked around. There were a couple of minor things broken and messed up, but overall it looked great. So we bought the house. We were so thrilled.

The day we moved in, I was helping the movers with some fireplace equipment. And when I put my foot on the hearth to step up, the whole thing just split open. Apparently, the previous owners who were sitting there during the inspection were covering up the crack in the mortar!

Lisa and I have owned several homes over the course of our marriage, and if you have ever bought a house, you know how important the home inspection is. A house can look great on the exterior, but it could be hiding some major foundation or plumbing issues.

It would be ludicrous to buy a house without first having an inspection. Yet, we get into things that are much more valuable than bricks and sticks in our lives. How often do we do a real inspection? When it comes to our relationships, we need to do THEY-inspections.

We need to inspect the character foundation—who a person is when no one is watching is who a person is. If they have a small issue now with lying, with self-control, or with discipline, there is a good chance that micro-issue will turn into a macro-issue down the road.

Here are some very practical questions you can

ask yourself as you're dating in order to determine if they truly are "the one."

- Do they have the kind of character you can live with for the next four or five decades?
- Do you want to become more like this person?
- Would you still want to marry them even if they never changed at all?
- Would you want this person to raise your children if something happened to you?

Also, inspect their relational history. How do they spell relational relief? Who are the "they" in their life? And do their "they" underscore and highlight great morals and values? If the person you are dating has a pattern of burning bridges in their past, who's to say that you won't be next in line?

Do not be misled: "Bad company corrupts good character."

—1 Corinthians 15:33

SHADE TWENTY-TWO:
OPEN HOUSE

Years ago Lisa and I were in Seoul, Korea, on a mission trip. While we were there, a missionary opened up her home to us. She welcomed us in for a meal, shared what she had, and treated us as special guests. It wasn't some grand home. She had a two-room home that was cramped and jammed. She didn't have a lot of furniture. She simply laid out a mat on the floor. But it was one of the greatest displays of hospitality I've ever seen. What she gave us that day is what you'll find in the right "they."

True hospitality is not about the lawn-mowing, house-showing mentality designed to impress the guests. It is expressed in the conversation-starting, love-imparting mentality designed to serve others. Entertainment says, "How does the house look?" Hospitality says, "How are you doing?"

You don't have to have a large home; look at our friend in Korea. You don't have to be a good cook; you can order a pizza. You don't even have to own a home; you can be hospitable at a diner or at a restaurant.

Our culture is always racing through routine, buried in business, tied to our technology. No wonder so many of our lives lack strong relationships. The right "they" hit the pause button to be a breath of fresh air in the lives of others.

Keep open house; be generous with your lives.
By opening up to others, you'll prompt people to
open up with God, this generous Father in heaven.
—Matthew 5:16 (msg)

SHADE TWENTY-THREE:
I'M A BIG HYPOCRITE

Have you ever seen those nametags that say, "Hi, my name is _____"? If we wore those stickers going into every relationship, but filled in the blank with the word "hypocrite," we could save our relationships a lot of shock, anger, and bitterness.

Let's face it. I am a big hypocrite and so are you. What is a hypocrite? It's someone who says one thing but does another. We all do that! We can't judge others because of it.

Jesus said in Matthew 7:3-5,

Why do you look at the speck of sawdust in your brother's eye and pay no attention to the plank in your own eye? How can you say to your brother, 'Let me take the speck out of your eye,' when all the time there is a plank in your own eye? You hypocrite, first take the plank out of your own eye,

and then you will see clearly to remove the speck
from your brother's eye.

Hypocrisy is simply wearing a mask. It comes from the Greek theater where actors would hold up different masks to represent different characters. But when you are honest about the mask you are wearing, you aren't worried about the mask slipping and being exposed. You can be your true self in the face of others.

I am big a hypocrite and so are you. And the right "they" realize the fact that they are hypocrites. The right "they" understand that, and when you do, you'll see clearer, judge less, and forgive more.

SHADE TWENTY-FOUR:
GREAT EXPECTATIONS

Hypocrisy is all about expectations. We will put on a mask because we think we know what others expect. But a healthy relational life doesn't come from guessing about expectations; it's found in having clear expectations.

Imagine you and I stood outside a room and I told you we were about to enter a prison cell. Then, when we entered, you saw a leather couch, worn but still in good condition, a flat-screen 30-inch TV, and an old but fully-functioning refrigerator in the corner. You would probably say, "Wow! This is nicer than I expected."

Now imagine right before we walked into that same room I told you we were about to enter the presidential suite at a five-star hotel. You would say, "This place is a dump!"

Expectations in relationships are game

changers. Many of us are constantly disappointed because "they" are not meeting our expectations; yet, we fail to realize that we are putting God-type pressure on human relationships. We do this with when we expect them to fulfill every one of our needs. And we do this to ourselves when we attempt to fulfill all the needs someone else may have.

Lisa and I have to communicate with one another about what our expectations are for our marriage. But, even on my best day, I'll never be able to meet all the needs—physical, emotional, psychological, spiritual—that Lisa, my children, my family, friends, or anyone else has. The only person who can fulfill our deepest needs is the one whose love is perfect. And that is Jesus.

I know what it is to be in need, and I know what it is to have plenty. I have learned the secret of being content in any and every situation, whether well fed or hungry, whether living in plenty or in want. I can do all this through him who gives me strength.
—Philippians 4:12-13

Look to God to do what only God can do, and

do not put that pressure on someone else. If your expectations aren't explained, or if they're too high, your "they" will let you down every time. Healthy expectations lead to healthy relationships. The right "they" communicate their expectations, they don't expect you to fulfill all their needs, and they don't try to meet every expectation that only God can meet.

SHADE TWENTY-FIVE: COMMITMENT

One unhealthy expectation that has developed in our world today is the expectation that there is always a way out. Our world is filled with prenuptial agreements, month-to-month apartment leases, and cell phone contracts with escape clauses. Why do we live in such a contract-driven world? Because commitment—real commitment—is a rare commodity. We would rather find a way out than a way through. And commitment is exactly what we need from those who are in our lives.

If the truth were known, most people in our world today have that decision-faking, work-shaking, vow-forgetting, job-quitting, church-hopping, spouse-shopping mentality that runs from commitment. We would rather bail out than blast through. We'd rather leave than last. We'd rather throw in the towel than stay in the game.

Before you invest relational capital into someone, you'd better research their commitment. Do they have a track record of bailing out when things get tough? Or are they the kind of person who sticks it out, no matter what? If you're not sure, they probably aren't. If they are a person of commitment, you'll see it. It's like a Las Vegas sign blinking, "Commitment!!" It's going to be obvious.

The Apostle Peter seemed like a man of commitment. He told Jesus, "I'm with you no matter what." But in Jesus' most desperate hour, when he needed Peter the most, Peter bailed on him. Peter lacked the commitment of the right "they." Later, Jesus reinstated him. But we can learn something powerful from Peter's lack of commitment in that moment. The right "they" are like an anchor that is not swayed by the changing tides of culture.

A man of too many friends comes to ruin, But there is a friend who sticks closer than a brother.
— Proverbs 18:24 (nasb),

Commitment is going all in; it's sticking to a position, no matter what the cost. Jesus was committed to you and to me. He went all in for us. The right "they" will be all in for us as well.

SHADE TWENTY-SIX:
TO BE OR NOT TO BE

Commitment is one of the most crucial aspects in any relationship, especially when it comes to the most important earthly relationship we can be part of: marriage.

"To be or not to be?" If they are someone you are dating, that is the question.

Waiting for Mr. or Mrs. Perfect to come along is waiting for something that does not exist. If you find someone you are attracted to and they love the Lord, have the right "they" in their life, have a consistent track record, and the right "they" in your life are all telling you, "Yes, this is the one," THEN JUST GET MARRIED!

If you are sexually involved and think marriage is the natural next step, I will tell you sex will no doubt cloud your judgment. If you want to make sure this is a person you intend to stay married to once you get married, then take a break from sex to clear your mind so you can evaluate each other objectively.

Marriage is not the easiest thing, but it is the greatest thing if you're willing to work! You have to have a strong marital work ethic and commitment to JUST STAY MARRIED. Have Lisa and I been "happily" married 24/7 throughout our entire marriage? No. Have there been more moments of happiness than I can count? Yes! Have we had a marriage worth fighting for every day? Without question! And would I be the man I am today without having had Lisa in my life sharpening me these past thirty-plus years? No chance. Together we strive to have a marriage that reflects God and points others to him.

Marriage is about our holiness, not our happiness. If that's not what you're looking for THEN JUST DON'T GET MARRIED!

Genesis 2:24 says,
That is why a man leaves his father and mother and is united to his wife, and they become one flesh.

Marriage is about becoming one flesh. It's a process. So really:

"To become or not to become?" THAT *is the question!*

SHADE TWENTY-SEVEN:
THE CONSTANCY OF CONSISTENCY

If I were a scout for a professional sports team and I had the choice between two athletes—one who just came off an impressive high scoring game but wasn't consistent in putting up those numbers on a regular basis, and the other a solid player with maybe lesser, but consistent numbers night after night—I would likely choose the second guy. What separates a good player from a great player? It's the ability to consistently put up twenty points per game rather than just having a hot hand every now and then.

Whether we are "scouting" for someone to marry, someone to date, someone to hire, or someone to be our friend, one thing we need to look for is the constancy of consistency.

The right "they" are consistent.

They understand the importance of consistency. They don't just have flashes of greatness. Anyone can put on a good show for a little while. Anyone can keep their nose clean for a little while. Anyone can be charming for a little while. But what about the long haul?

At Fellowship Church, we've been blessed with some amazing staff members—those who have been consistent in their love for the church, their commitment to the ministry, and their drive to reach the lost. Several of our staff members have been at the church for more than a decade. They have shown more than a flash of greatness; they've shown consistent performance, game in and game out.

If you wonder about the people in your life, look at their career. Do you see consistency? Look at their past relationships. Do you see consistency? Look at their decisions and choices. Do you see consistency? Look at what they post on social media. Do you see consistency? Think about how they treat you. Do you see the consistency?

If there isn't consistency, then you might run into a relational emergency one day. The right "they" are consistent.

SHADE TWENTY-EIGHT: GRASSHOPPERS OR GIANT BOPPERS

When I think of consistency I think of one of my favorite stories in the Bible that is found in Exodus. It's all about the Israelites who had been led miraculously out of slavery. On their journey, God consistently performed miracles starting with the miracles that led to their release from slavery, to the parting of the Red Sea so they could cross on dry land, to providing them with manna (the cosmic carbohydrate that came from the sky), to guiding them with a cloud by day and a pillar of fire by night, and to providing water that flowed out of a rock when they were thirsty. It was an amazing journey! Finally, they found themselves on the outskirts of the Promised Land in a place called Kadesh.

Their leader, Moses, sent twelve spies into the land to scope it out. When they returned, their report started off great, but then something happened. Ten of the twelve spies went negative. They started to doubt God's promise that they could take the land and they put people's opinions over God's. Rather than remembering all God had done for them, all he was capable of, they allowed fear, doubt, and negativity to sink in and said, "The people there are giants and we are nothing but grasshoppers in their eyes."

I researched grasshoppers. And there are some dangerous qualities about grasshoppers that, if we allow them into our lives, can cause us some serious pain. Check this out.

First of all, grasshoppers are destructive. They cost us $1.5 billion a year in damaged crops. The ears of a grasshopper are on their abdomen, so they are deaf to many sounds. They have their ears to the ground. And, what do negative people do? They have their ear to the ground and listen to everyone's opinion.

Also, grasshoppers jump and fly from place to place to place. If we were grasshoppers, we could jump 100 yards. Grasshopper people are disloyal.

They jump from team to team, relationship to relationship, job to job, church to church.

Grasshoppers are also defensive. They spit that brown, tobacco-looking juice at you. Negative people—grasshopper people—will spit and vomit that negativity at everyone they come into contact with.

We can't surround ourselves with grasshoppers; we need to surround ourselves with giant boppers!

Then Caleb silenced the people before Moses and said, "We should go up and take possession of the land, for we can certainly do it."
—Numbers 13:30

Caleb and Joshua (the other two of the twelve spies) were giant boppers! They said, "We can do this!" They were the right "they."

Are you surrounded by grasshoppers or giant boppers? The right "they" are giant boppers. Even if their initial thoughts are, "I'm not good enough, I'm not strong enough, I'm not smart enough," in the end, they know God is always God enough and they move forward with optimism and courage, caring more about the opinion of God than the opinion of others.

SHADE TWENTY-NINE: WHY NOT?

Have you ever been presented with an opportunity, like the Israelites faced in Kadesh, only to then be confronted with some kind of struggle to reach it? We all have. The fact is there is no opportunity without opposition.

A friend of mine had a great opportunity to move to a new city, to help start an amazing ministry. The difficulty was that in order to do it, he had to pick up and leave everything he was familiar with, and even let go of another good opportunity outside of ministry. But my friend knew this was the opportunity God wanted him to take. The problem was, nearly everyone he knew kept asking him, "Why? Why would you leave your home and everything you know? Why would you leave your friends for something that is unknown? Why? Why? Why?"

Think about that question: "Why?" It sounds a lot like whine, doesn't it? The question "Why?" isn't a bad question if it's designed to help motivate someone to find what God has for them. The right "they" ask "Why?" but then follow it up with another significant word, and ask "Why not?"

An unhealthy why is merely whining. A healthy why is "Why not?"

"Why not take this risk? Why not make this commitment? Why not step out in faith and trust? Why not? Why not? Why not?!"

The right "they" don't need an explanation for every decision you make. They trust. They follow. Rather than asking, "Why?" They ask, "Why not?" And they help you examine all the possibilities of what could become of it.

If you have to constantly explain and defend yourself for every chance you take, then you're talking to the wrong "they"; and they are slowing you down from going where God wants to take you in life. Instead, find those who are asking, "Why not?" and experience the amazing trajectory God has for you!

SHADE THIRTY: MANAGERS, NOT OWNERS

The right "they" are "Why not?" people in every area of their lives. This is why you'll find one of the greatest qualities in the right "they"—generosity—because generosity is all about asking, "Why not?"

The right "they" know that a life of generosity is all about living the way God has designed us to live, and that when it comes to money, we are managers and not owners. The right "they" know that when they properly manage the things God has given them, they can live a life of generosity. They have things, but things don't have them. And because of that, they have a spirit of generosity. That doesn't mean they are necessarily wealthy; a spirit of generosity has nothing to do with your net worth. It's all about a mindset.

Unlike the wrong "they" who have a poverty mentality and think they have to hold onto everything tightly, the right "they" have a generosity mentality and understand that it is better to give than to receive. Both are contagious. The question is, which one are you going to catch?

Also, we are called to manage it well. Everything we have comes from God. And the Bible tells us we're to return the first ten percent of all we make to God through the local church. And when we live that way and put God first in our finances, he promises to bless us.

Imagine that I went away and left three people with a thousand dollars each to feed and watch after my family. When I returned, I found that the first person saved the majority of the money, but my family was not well fed. The second person spent the entire amount, but clearly not on my family. And finally, the third person had carefully spent all the money in a way where my family was well fed and provided for. Who am I more likely to hire the next time around and trust to handle my resources?

Generosity begins by understanding that

everything we have comes from God. And when we give the first ten percent back to him (the tithe), he promises to bless our lives in return.

"Bring all the tithes into the storehouse so there will be enough food in my Temple. If you do," says the Lord of Heaven's Armies, "I will open the windows of heaven for you. I will pour out a blessing so great you won't have enough room to take it in! Try it! Put me to the test!"

—Malachi 3:10 (NLT)

Do you want God to bless your relationships? Be someone who understands the fact that your stuff is not your stuff. And link up with the right "they," who understand that we are blessed to be a blessing.

SHADE THIRTY-ONE:
RHYTHM

In the fast paced, easily accessible, and non-stop world we live in, something that is becoming equally as valuable to how we manage money is how we manage time. Everyone is looking for "balance." But there is no such thing as balance. As soon as you start succeeding in one area, you begin suffering in another. What we need is not balance; it's rhythm.

God has a rhythm for our lives, and it goes like this: 1, 2, 3, 4, 5, 6, rest. In Genesis 1, we read that God worked for six days, and then when the masterpiece was complete, he pushed back and rested on the seventh. 1, 2, 3, 4, 5, 6, rest.

Lisa and I work hard, but we rest hard too. We rest weekly by giving God our first, the Sabbath, the day of rest. We stop working and we go to church as a family to recharge and be refreshed.

We regularly take breaks because we've learned that if you don't take a break from your schedule, your schedule will break you.

> *Remember the Sabbath day by keeping it holy.*
> —Exodus 20:8

We all need that day of rest, not just to stop working, but so we can recharge. And nothing will recharge your life like time in God's House. That's what the Sabbath is all about.

The right they understand the need to stop every now and then and do those things that refresh us. It's when we are relaxed that our minds are at ease and the theta waves can begin to crash on the coastline of our consciousness, giving us the fuel and energy to experience life the way God wants us to.

When was the last time you did something that refreshes you? When was the last time you took a break? When was the last time you went on a vacation?

Married couples, you need to take those weekly breaks (date nights) to reconnect with one another. Get away together for a vacation at least once a year, even if that means going somewhere inexpensive and local. Spouses, a vacation means taking time to get away with just the two of you. It's not a family trip. A family trip is great, but nothing will refuel your marriage like time away with just the two of you.

Match your rhythm to the rhythm God has set, and follow the rhythm of the right "they": 1, 2, 3, 4, 5, 6, rest.

SHADE THIRTY-TWO: WATCH THE WORK

God's rhythm of "1, 2, 3, 4, 5, 6, rest" shows us not only the importance of rest, but also the importance of work! God models work. Before sin ever entered the world, he gave us responsibilities and told man to work and take care of the earth. Most people shirk when they think about work, but work can be a good thing when we realize work is a God thing.

Whatever you do, work at it with all your heart, as working for the Lord.
—Colossians 3:23

It's clear so far that relationships take work. The need to forgive, the work to overcome anger, the drive to work through difficulty—it all takes work. And that's the real secret to a great relationship. Work!

If you want to get better at your golf swing, your education, your interior decorating skills, or anything else in life, it takes work. Relationships are not any different and the right "they" are willing to work! They work on communicating, on listening, on understanding, on serving, on strengthening areas of weakness. Watch the work of those around you and you'll see the right "they" stand out.

One of the greatest love stories of all time is found in the Bible between a man named Boaz and a woman named Ruth. Ruth and her mother-in-law Naomi had both lost their husbands. Instead of just sitting around, sulking over the loss of her husband, Ruth made a commitment to help Naomi survive, so she went out into the wheat fields, found a job, and worked at collecting grain. It was there that she caught the eye of the owner of the fields, billionaire Boaz. And what caught his eye about Ruth were two things: her beauty and her work ethic.

I would be lying if I said the first thing that attracted me to Lisa when I was fifteen years old was her work ethic. But after a while, I began to see what a hard worker she was (and is). That kind of work ethic and tenacity has translated into our marriage over the past 32-plus years. No laziness, no entitlement.

Relationships take work. And the right "they" in your life are willing to work—inside the relationship and outside of the relationship!

SHADE THIRTY-THREE: LAUGH

Have you ever noticed we all have a fake laugh? It's hilarious. I'm sure you know the difference between your real laugh and your fake laugh. Not only does it sound different, but it produces something different in you as well. The right "they" will bring out the real laugh in you.

One of the most difficult and stressful things I do is public speaking. Inevitably people ask, "Do you get nervous before you speak?" And I can see the shock in their eyes when I answer them because I know they expect me to say "No." There's serious pressure in getting up every weekend in front of a lot of people and communicating, hopefully in a creative and compelling way, God's plan and purpose for our lives.

So what do I do? I laugh with (and sometimes at) friends. (Women laugh with their friends. Guys laugh at their friends.) I'll sometimes pick up the phone, call my close friends and we'll just laugh. I spend time with Lisa and we laugh. I even laugh at myself.

Some of our best ideas over the history of Fellowship have been the result of laughter. When you laugh your real laugh, your mind begins to work in ways it can't otherwise.

They say (there's that phrase again) that laughter is the best medicine. But that's not just a catchy saying. There's some serious truth to it. When we laugh, endorphins are released. There's a physiological response. Stress reduces and our blood pressure drops.

So we have to laugh. We should laugh. When we surround ourselves with people we can laugh with, we discover affirmation. We find our self-esteem rising. Laughter breaks down barriers. So make sure you are finding those you can laugh with!

> *A cheerful heart is good medicine.*
> —Proverbs 17:22

SHADE THIRTY-FOUR:
UNDER THE UMBRELLA

You want a good laugh? Picture someone in a rainstorm holding an opened umbrella, not above them, but beside them, exposing themselves to all the elements. That would be ridiculous wouldn't it?

Life can be a storm that drenches us with dysfunction, pelts us with problems, and hammers us with hell—that is, if we are not standing under the umbrella of authority God has placed in our lives.

God is a God of authority and he has given us an umbrella of authority to get under, where we can experience the protection and provision our lives need. The Bible teaches us that God has placed different types of authority figures—leaders— over us in life to provide order and growth.

The right "they" understand that the authorities

in their lives are placed there to shape them and mold them into diamonds. We're all diamonds in the rough. Leaders are there to excavate us, chip away the imperfections, and help shape us into beautiful diamonds. It's sometimes a difficult process. It's not always comfortable. We may not even always like those who are in authority over us.

People say, "I can't submit to that person until I respect them;" but, if you're waiting to respect the person, you'll never get there. We have to respect the position and submit to their authority in our lives. The right "they" find and know their link in God's chain of command.

The problem is, I don't think I've ever met someone who has said, "I love it when I don't get my way and am challenged to do something I don't naturally want to do!"

In the Old Testament, King Saul came across this problem. He was preparing for battle, and God's man, Samuel, told the king to wait for him to make the sacrifices before the battle. But selfish Saul grew impatient waiting for Samuel to show up. So what did he do? He bucked the authority and did things his own way. He made the decision to make sacrifices without Samuel's presence.

While the fires were still smoldering, take a wild stab at who showed up. The man of God, the prophet of God: Samuel.

Samuel asked Saul, "What have you done?" Check out Saul's response.

When I saw that the men were scattering, and that you did not come at the set time, and that the Philistines were assembling at Mikmash, I thought, "Now the Philistines will come down against me at Gilgal, and I have not sought the Lord's favor." So I felt compelled to offer the burnt offering.

—1 Samuel 13:11-12

I saw. I thought. I felt. Three steps that we all take when we go against the authority in our lives.

Deep down, we all have authority issues. But the right "they" understand the powerful truth that when we get under those things God has placed over us, we can get over those things God has placed under us. They know and understand their link in the chain of God's command.

As our response to authority outside a relationship goes, so goes our response to authority inside a relationship. If you have a "they" in your life that is always going negative and doing the push back to the leadership God has placed in their lives, then you are dealing with someone who thinks they know it all, and they are not coachable and moldable. That ride of pride will eventually steam right on through into your relationship as well. But the right "they" understand this whole authority thing.

The right "they" are umbrella fellas and princesses of parasols.

SHADE THIRTY-FIVE: WHAT THE HECKNOLOGY

We all have that tendency to do our own thing, don't we? We want to hold our own umbrellas the way we want to hold them. It's all about us. And it doesn't help that in today's world, social media is everywhere. And social media, if we're not careful becomes social ME-dia, pumping up our pride and incubating our insecurities.

In essence, we're creating a culture of narcissists.

Jean Twenge and Keith Campbell, two noted sociologists and authors of *The Narcissism Epidemic***, wrote:

> *Understanding the narcissism epidemic is important, because its long-term*

consequences are destructive to society. American culture's focus on self-admiration has caused a flight from reality to the land of grandiose fantasy. Permissive parenting, celebrity culture, and the internet are among the causes of the emerging narcissism epidemic.

What's it all mean? We're into highlight reel living. And it definitely engages the engines of envy. We look at someone's posts and think, "Wow, look at their life. Look at the parties they attend, the places they travel, the opportunities they have. Must be nice!"

If you want to feel like you're not doing much, go on social media and peruse the pages and posts. It's all about the way people spin it and the way we perceive it. Again, it's highlight reel living.

What is social media really about anyway? It's all about pride. Yet, most people don't realize they are prideful. I've never met someone who admitted, "Yes, I struggle with pride." Yet that pride parade and those engines of envy can all get revved up based on who we follow and what we look at with social media.

Do you follow the right "they" on social media? Or are you following the kind of characters that pull you away from God's plan for you? Are you maybe following some of these people?:

- **Hal Humility** – This is the person who is prideful in their humility, who promotes their lowliness in spirit, who brags and then throws in words like "humbled" and "blessed." So often we're prideful in our humility and humble in our pride.
- **Dana Destination** – She's always promoting another travel spot, reminding you: "I'm here and you're not."
- **Tim Trophy.** – He loves to post photo after photo of his accomplishments. Maybe he throws in a picture of him with a celebrity or he tells you all about his trophy friends.
- **Susan Selfie** – Every picture is the same. When she takes a picture or posts a comment, the focus is always on her.
- **Paula Party** – She's always at a party making you think, "Why didn't I get invited? I guess I don't have as many friends as she does."

- **Sam Soapbox** – He hyper focuses on one issue and never lets it go. Every post is a rant about the same thing.
- **Barbara Bikini** – She loves to get the lust engines going. She posts photos of herself in a bikini, but then she'll throw up a random Bible verse attached to it.
- **Ed Ego** – He knows how to crop the photo, add a filter to it, and make everything about it just right to make him look like he is the MAN and you are not.

Be careful following these people! Are you following the right "they" on social media?

Make sure you checknology before you wrecknology!

SHADE THIRTY-SIX: DON'T BAIL OUT BEFORE THE BREAKTHROUGH

Years ago I had the opportunity to run a marathon. A friend of mine, who was an avid runner, gave me one warning. He said, "Around the eighteen to twenty-mile marker you'll hit a wall and your body will want to shut down."

I naively thought, "I'm in good shape, I'll be fine." But sure enough, I hit that twenty-mile marker and my body started to shut down. I hit the wall. But then something amazing happened. My friend came out onto the course and ran alongside me for the last several miles, cheering me on and coaching me through the finish.

Have you ever hit a wall? Not in a marathon, but in your relationships? Have you ever felt as though things were shutting down and you wanted to throw in the towel? Are you there right now, wanting to quit and no one knows it but you? What do you do when quitting seems better than crashing through?

Walls are normal; every relationship deals with them. In marriage you'll face monotony. In dating relationships, you're going to face differences. There will be seasons of your life where it doesn't seem like much is happening. It's not hot. It's not cold. It's just bland and lukewarm. Don't quit!

I can promise you from years of working with people, if you bail on this relationship, you'll bail on the next. Don't bail before the breakthrough. God wants more for you than a trail of broken relationships. And like my friend at the marathon, Jesus is right there running alongside you, coaching you through those quitting points, and helping you reach the finish line.

The right "they" are there to run alongside you as well, cheering you on to reach your goal.

SHADE THIRTY-SEVEN: BRINGING HONOR BACK

In the marathon of life, the right "they" are easy to spot. They stand out because they are people of honor. But we live in a culture, a dimension that too often honors dishonor and dishonors honor.

What does it mean to dishonor someone? It means to treat that person as common. You won't find the right "they" in this dimension. Because they understand that you will never lock eyes with someone who does not matter to God. We are all special and unique. The right "they" treat everyone that way.

To find the right "they" you have to go to an honorable dimension. This dimension starts with honoring God with our words as well as our actions. It's a dimension where we detach ourselves from conversations that descend into dishonor and gravitate toward those that honor others. It's a dimension where we decide we will honor the position if we can't honor the person.

This dimension is where we develop a new language with words like "Thank you," "I appreciate you," "How may I help you," "Yes Sir", "Yes Ma'am." No, this isn't a foreign language; it's the language of honor.

This really hit home in my life a while back when my Uncle Blake died. Uncle Blake was a peculiar person, a unique individual, highly complex, highly generous. He gave his life for the things of God. We gathered together in that tiny town in South Carolina, sitting around in different restaurants, at the funeral home, during the wake, during the funeral, on the way back to the airport. And all we were doing was honoring Uncle Blake. We were sharing funny stories, talking about what he meant to us. And to hear all of the people discuss his life and their honorable words; that was something to behold.

It's sad, isn't it, that too many of us wait until it's too late to truly give honor to the people in our lives. Honor is the feng shui of relationships.

It brings order and helps everything fit in its right place so it pops. If you want a life that pops, then surround yourself with the right "they," take it to that honorable dimension, and together let's bring honor back!

The right "they" will honor up, honor down, and honor all around!

The wise inherit honor, but fools get only shame.
—Proverbs 3:35

SHADE THIRTY-EIGHT: CREATIVITY

There are many things we can learn from God about characteristics of the right "they," but one of those that he has put on display from the beginning of time might go overlooked: creativity. It's the fifth word in the Bible!

> *In the beginning, God created . . .*
> —Genesis 1:1

God invented creativity. Jesus modeled it. The Holy Spirit empowers it. And people need it!

A sunrise, a sunset, the breeze over the ocean, the look in the eyes of a loved one, or a divine and perfectly designed orchestrated occurrence in our lives; God's creativity is alive, bringing life to our relationships with him and with others; it's constantly refreshing, awakening, and inspiring us.

The right "they" understand their creativity.

They realize that we're all creative because we were made in the image of our creative Creator. The question we need to be asking isn't, "How do I become creative?" The question is, "What are the barriers that are keeping me from becoming creative?"

Creativity is vital in every relationship. Too often we get a creative cramp because of complacency. We can get stuck in the shallows of sameness as opposed to riding on the ragged edge of creativity.

Romance is merely creativity that stems from honor. If I see Lisa as uncommon (which is the definition of honor), then I am amazed and grateful for my relationship with her and I want to express that in a way that translates my gratitude—thus, creativity follows.

The right "they" are creative. I'm not necessarily talking about painting canvases or writing poems and songs; but, rather than going through the same mundane routine, the right "they" keep it fresh and exciting, because they see YOU as uncommon. They will be creative for you, because they see value in you.

SHADE THIRTY-NINE: CHANGE – CONFLICT – GROWTH

Creativity is all about change, and sometimes change has to happen in your relationships. Maybe by now you realize that certain people in your life are not the right "they."

If you are at a crossroads, talk to someone. Talk to the right "they." If it's a more serious matter, talk with a trusted pastor or Christian counselor. But no matter the degree of change that you know you need to make, change is never easy; because where there is change, there will be conflict.

Change requires us to alter some things. Sometimes it's a mindset. Other times it's our circumstances. Sometimes it requires us to stop hanging out with certain people or going to certain places, and that can cause some hurt feelings and some conflict. But I have learned something powerful. On the other side of that conflict is always growth. It's the spin cycle of true success: Change – Conflict – Growth.

Perhaps you have been in a dating relationship for quite some time and the "natural" next step is marriage, but something has held you back and now you know what it is. They aren't the right "they." Change is never easy, but heartbreak that lasts for a little while is better than a mistake that lasts a lifetime.

Maybe it's become apparent to you that a certain set of friends you run with are not the right "they" and the fear of losing popularity and no longer being a part of a certain crowd have you frozen. Do you want popularity or purpose? Make the changes you need to make in order to experience what God wants you to experience.

Change is brutiful. It can be brutal to go through, but what awaits you on the others side is beautiful!

Don't fear that brutiful change! Get in on the spin cycle of success: Change – Conflict – Growth.

SHADE FORTY:
QUESTIONS

People who know me know that I love to ask questions. As a child, I remember people saying to me, "Ed, you ask too many questions." I think it must be genetic, too. When our children were younger, we would take road trips, and they would ask so many questions that Lisa and I would have to place question quotas on them. We would tell them all, "You have a limit of three questions."

I wish that as children grew, they would continue to ask questions, because questions are crucial. Questions are important. When we ASK we are Always Seeking Knowledge (ASK). The greatest way to learn is by asking questions. Think about it. When you are reading something, what are you really doing? You're asking a question. When you listen to a speaker, you're asking questions. "What does this person have to communicate? How can I relate this to my life? What can I learn from this moment?"

I've learned if you want to get somewhere in life you have to ask the right people the right questions in order to get the right answers.

Ask the right people: Are you surrounding yourself with people who are moving forward or are already at the place you want to be? If I have a question about fishing, I'm not going to go to a golf expert. And, I would not ask someone about a challenge in my marriage unless they had been married for many years and were still committed to their marriage.

Ask the right questions: The right questions are usually not the easiest, because they require thought and vulnerability. They force you to admit, "I don't know it all." Too often, we stop asking questions out of fear. But what some might perceive as a weakness, the Bible teaches us is a powerful strength:

> *When pride comes, then comes disgrace, but with humility comes wisdom.*
> —Proverbs 11:2

Here are three profound questions to begin asking as you seek out the right "they":

- "What do I need to CREATE in my life?" Is there something I haven't been doing that I should start doing?
- "What do I need to CANCEL in my life?" Is there something I have been doing that I need to stop doing?
- "What does this information I've learned CONFIRM in my life?" Is there something I have been doing that I need to continue doing?

If we're going to get the right answers in life then we need to be asking the right questions to the right people. That means our inner circle needs to be made up of incurable learners—people who constantly ask questions because the right "they" master the task of the ASK.

SHADE FORTY-ONE:
GOOD 'N' ANGRY

Here's a question: How do you process anger? The way we handle anger says a lot about whether or not they are the right "they."

Some people handle anger "Tupperware" style. Instead of coming clean and dealing with it right away, they put their anger and resentment in a container, secure the top on the container, shelve it, and allow their frosty feelings to fester. But after a while a putrid odor begins to permeate the atmosphere. And when the container is opened, the stench knocks everyone to their knees!

Some people deal with anger "Frappuccino" style. They just ice everyone out. But those frozen feelings can numb the situation for a while. But eventually, the situation becomes even worse.

Some deal with anger "Gun-slinger" style. The slightest conflict and they start shooting words of anger at everyone around.

Anger is not necessarily a bad thing; it's neutral. What separates good anger from toxic anger is what we get angry about and how we deal with our anger. The right "they" know how to properly process their anger.

The Bible says in Ephesians 4:26-27,

"In your anger do not sin": Do not let the sun go down while you are still angry, and do not give the devil a foothold.

I remember a while back someone did something to me that made me hot with anger. All I wanted to do in that moment was call them and uncage my rage. Fortunately, the Holy Spirit of God gave me the discernment to wait, to talk it through with the right "they" in my life, and then make the call after I cooled off. So I did. And when I eventually called this person, the anger was still there, but I was able to process and communicate it in a way that was edifying and not electrifying.

Usually anger is a secondary emotion. We don't want to feel the first emotion so we just jump to anger. In the Old Testament, Saul became jealous of David. But rather than dealing with his jealousy, Saul jumped straight to anger and tried to kill David.

The right "they" don't take action on their first reaction. They don't let the sun go down on their anger and give the devil even a toehold. They get angry, but they get angry about the right things and handle it the right way.

SHADE FORTY-TWO: WAKE UP!

You know what makes a lot of pastors and preachers good 'n' angry? Sleeping in church.

There's a story in the Bible all about the first person ever to get caught sleeping in church. One night, when the church was gathering, a young man named Eutychus found a really comfortable spot on a windowsill to listen to the Apostle Paul preach.

Now back in the days of the early church, they didn't put a countdown clock on the services. Time just flowed and they were in it for the long haul. The Bible says that Paul continued his message until after midnight.

As he was hearing Paul talk on and on, Eutychus began to fall into a deep sleep. Then something startled him, he fell out of the window, dropped three stories, and hit the pavement.

Everyone thought, "There's nothing we can do. He's dead!" Paul stopped his message, ran down three flights of stairs, embraced Eutychus, brought the guy back to life, and then led him back up three flights of stairs and continued preaching into the wee hours of the morning. Wow! Eutychus was sleeping in church; he was asleep to the purpose God had for him. What Eutychus needed was to WAKE UP!

Satan, who the Bible says roams the earth like a lion looking for prey to devour, preys on our relationships in the most unassuming way: with nursery rhymes and lullabies. He tries to lull us to sleep so that we begin to hit the snooze button on things like integrity, discipline, communication, creativity. He sweetly sings to you and me this nursery rhyme:

"Rock-a-bye believer in the tree top,
Snoozing will cause your influence to stop.
Ignore the alarm, stay in bed,
Say no to the right people,
You'll soon be dead."

Satan tries to get us to drink decaf coffee and

slowly drift off to sleep. But life is too short for decaf coffee. What we need is to WAKE UP! And the alarm clock reads 5:14!

Wake up, sleeper, rise from the dead, and Christ will shine on you.
—Ephesians 5:14

The right "they" are people who caffeinate you! Like shots of espresso, we need people in our lives who wake us up!

There is one place you will find the right "they" who will caffeinate your life and where those relationships will be re-caffeinated again and again. That place is the local church. It's not just that they are at church; they are in the church. They are consistent and contributing, not complaining and consuming.

My greatest friends over the years have been people who understand if you are not serving you're swerving. They are not church shoppers and hoppers, not drive-through Christians; they are people who get the fact that "it's not about me; it's about He and others."

Talk about relationships that wake you up to

God's purpose for your life! The right "they" are there to wake you up!

SHADE FORTY-THREE: ROLLS ROYCE DOESN'T ADVERTISE

A while back I was at a high school basketball game with some friends who had a son on the team. I was sitting beside the father of one of the star players on the court, and as the game progressed I could see that this kid was really good. I asked his father, "Hey is your son doing a lot of AAU stuff, basketball camps, or club teams to get colleges interested in recruiting him?"

He said, "No."

Shocked, I said, "Really?"

Then he said something that I'll never forget. He said, "You know what I believe? I believe if you're good enough, they'll find you."

What a statement! If you're good enough, they'll find you. How true that is! But in our world, especially with the pervasion of social media, too many people think they have to self-promote to the point of saturation. My Australian friends call it being a "try hard."

The right "they" don't have to try hard to promote themselves.

Have you ever seen a commercial for a Rolls Royce? If so, it's very rare. Do you know why? Because Rolls Royce doesn't have to advertise.

If "they" are constantly having to tell you who they are, what they are about; if they are constantly dropping names like they have something prove, you have to wonder if it's all smoke and mirrors.

The fruit of the Spirit is love, joy, peace, forbearance, kindness, goodness, faithfulness, gentleness and self-control.
—Galatians 5:22-23

Actions speak louder than words. Regardless of who they say they are, do you see a love for God and for others? Do they have outrageous and contagious joy? When there is a problem do they initiate reconciliation to bring about peace? Are they patient? Do they have the kindness of the Lord? Do you see goodness, morality, and purity in their lives? Are they faithful? Are they committed, pledging themselves no matter the cost? Are they self-controlled? If so, it'll show. They don't have to promote themselves constantly.

The right "they" are like a Rolls Royce. They don't need to advertise because a Rolls is a Rolls!

SHADE FORTY-FOUR:
YOU BE YOU

We've been asking the question, "Who are they?" But here's another question: "Who are YOU?"

When you know who you are and whose you are, you don't have to advertise yourself to the world. Like my friend in the previous chapter, you know your skills and you know your talent. And you let the game come to you.

We all are looking for an identity. But in that search, too many surround themselves with people who try to change them to be something they were never created to be. Are you able to be the real you around the people in your life?

We need to get our primary props from God. Our self-esteem is based on who God has created us to be. It's been said that having a great self-esteem is seeing yourself the way God sees you, nothing more nothing less. However, we're relational creatures, so our secondary props need to come from those who celebrate us for being us.

We have to be surrounded by the right "they" who point us back to God. And we need to find people in our lives who encourage us to be who God has created us to be!

The right "they" accept us as we are.

I'm not saying they don't challenge or sharpen us, but if you have to constantly work to get someone to merely accept you, it's not worth it; it's exhausting.

God made us unique and one of a kind. Psalm 139 in the Bible says that you were fearfully and wonderfully made by God.

When I get to heaven one day, God won't ask me, "Ed, why weren't you more like so-and-so?" No, He'll say, "Ed, why weren't you more like YOU?"

If I try to be someone I am not, there will be a hole in history, a gap in God's creative order. No one else can be me, and no one else can be you. The right "they" understand that, and they celebrate it.

YOU be YOU and surround yourself with the right "they" who help make that possible!

SHADE FORTY-FIVE: DRAWBRIDGE

Like Psalm 139 says, you were fearfully and wonderfully made. Your life is one of God's greatest creations. Think of it like a castle. Castles are beautiful structures. Each one built is unique. If you travel throughout Europe, you can still visit many of the medieval castles that were constructed centuries ago. They are typically built high on a hill, surrounded by walls and towers, and often encircled by a moat. To get across the moat and into the castle, a drawbridge has to be let down.

Back in the day, when the enemy was approaching, trumpets would sound, everyone would come into the safety of the castle, and the drawbridge would be pulled back up. With the bridge up, everything was secure. It was only by letting down that drawbridge that someone could get inside.

Many of us have our drawbridge up, shutting everyone out, and it gives us a false sense of security. We don't realize having our drawbridge up is harmful though it might appear helpful to our lives.

Yes, we do need to be wise about who we let our walls down for, but we all need those people in our lives we can let our guard down for and who we can be one hundred percent open and vulnerable to. We need people we can go to for help and advice. We can't live every minute of every day acting as if we have it all figured out. We cannot do life all on our own strength and wisdom. We need people with whom we can admit our weaknesses and share our struggles—people who can hold us accountable.

Accountability is a dangerous word, though, because many do not understand what it means. Real accountability emerges out of affinity. It is built out of love and understanding. We need people who will hold us accountable, people we can trust to have our best in mind.

How do you know if your "they" are someone

you can trust and let your drawbridge down for? Do they have their drawbridge down to anyone and everyone? Are they sharing details that were shared with them in confidence from someone else's life? Is this someone who has stood by your side long enough to prove they are a "with you" type of person? Are they the right "they": tough, honest, encouraging, and yielded?

> *As iron sharpens iron, so one person sharpens another.*
> —Proverbs 27:17

Lower your drawbridge for the right "they" so they can come into your life and truly sharpen you.

SHADE FORTY-SIX:
SPEAK THE TRUTH IN LOVE

Part of letting your guard down to the right "they" is opening ourselves up for constructive critique. Let's be real, though. We all like to hear what makes us feel better about ourselves. But a person who only tells you what you want to hear is no friend at all. They are what I call sinful sympathizers. They comfort our choices rather than challenge us to make better ones.

We can surround ourselves with people like this all day long if it makes us feel better about ourselves. But in the end, that kind of relationship hurts us more than we realize. We may feel better for the moment, but we won't be better in the long run.

*A lying tongue hates those it hurts, and a
flattering mouth works ruin.*

—Proverbs 26:28

Every Saturday night at church, after my first sermon for the weekend, I meet with a team to critique everything that happened. This is where we adjust and tweak the message and the entire weekend experience to meet our own expectations. Many times, this is a tough meeting. It's not always easy to hear what could have been better. But I am always better for having these critique sessions. The critique is never personal; it's purposeful. It isn't critical; it's constructive.

The right "they" speak the truth in love.

Rather than being sinful sympathizers, they are encouraging empathizers who love us enough to tell us the truth. They don't point their finger, but rather lend us their hand.

SHADE FORTY-SEVEN: RESCUE RADICALLY

One day I was in a little boat, a 16-footer, in the Atlantic Ocean with my friend Beau. We had a pretty intense day of fishing, and as we finished, we headed toward the marina. We could actually see the marina. No one else was anywhere near us. Then we looked across the water and saw a little craft out in the deep. And as we looked closer, we could see someone that looked like they were swimming about 150 feet behind the boat.

My friend said, "That's weird. What's someone doing swimming in shark infested waters? Why is someone in the water at this time of night? Let's go over and see what the deal is."

As we approached them we saw this guy waving to us. Then we realized he was in trouble. Between gasps of air he called out, "I've been treading water for twenty minutes. I'm about to go down. Please help!"

This guy was a leviathan. He was about 6'4" and weighed probably 230 pounds. We idled up to him. And I grabbed one of his hands, my friend grabbed the other, and we pulled this guy into the boat. As we pulled him over the side, the boat was taking on water, and we were struggling to get him in. It was a sight! Finally we got the guy on board, and after he caught his breath, while he was on his hands and knees, he was thanking us and coughing up salt water and just going on and on.

We asked him what happened and he said, "Well, I'm a commercial fisherman. I was by myself. I tripped and went overboard. As I turned to grab the railing of the boat, the wind pushed the boat out of my reach and I was trying to catch the boat, but now I've just been treading water." Then he said, "You saved my life! Thank you, thank you, thank you!"

After he regained his composure, we took him to his boat, and then we turned and made our way toward the marina.

Even though this book focuses on finding the right "they," make sure you don't mistake that for meaning we ought to isolate ourselves and live in some kind of a bubble. Don't think we should just stay in our little boat with our Christian friends and sing Christian songs while using Christian fishing poles. Don't think we're called to ignore everything going on around us.

One of the most common phrases used to describe Jesus was "friend of sinners." His closest friends were the right "they," but he was also constantly rubbing shoulders with people who did not have the right "they" in their lives. He was on a constant search and rescue mission to pull people out of the depths of their depravity and sin.

God has placed people in your life and in mine who are flailing around in deep water, clinging desperately to poor flotation devices and they need you to throw them the life ring: Jesus.

The right "they" know that the RING is the THING. They have been radically rescued and they know they are called to rescue radically.

SHADE FORTY-EIGHT:
PRAY

Relationships are all about one another. Whether it's rescuing a leviathan who is drowning in the ocean, helping a friend navigate through a difficult decision in their life, or serving your spouse to show them how appreciated they are, it's all about one another.

And if you're going to have the octane to do all those things, if you're going to see God do what you could never do on your own, then you're going to need to invite him into those relationships. And how do you do that? You pray.

The idea of prayer intimidates a lot of people. But prayer isn't some mystical exercise designed for the super spiritual. It's simply having a conversation with God. One of the biggest concerns of our technology-driven world is syncing up.

Prayer is syncing up with God.

The right "they" will pray, and pray continually, because they want their relationship with God to grow and thrive. They will also continually pray for you, because they want our relationship with God to grow and thrive.

Prayer is crucial in our relationships with others. What if a relationship seems completely hopeless and beyond repair? What if it seems impossible for someone to change? What if you have trouble finding and connecting with the right "they"? What should you do? Pray.

Over the years I have seen prayer move the hand of God in miraculous ways. One of the most powerful, high-risk prayers I ever prayed was years ago when I was in college.

I was twenty years old and a sophomore at Florida State University. I knelt down in our athletic dorm, rested my elbows on the air conditioning unit, looked out over a darkened parking lot, and said these words, "God, help me to point someone to you tomorrow." That's exactly what I prayed.

The next day, I was walking to class with one of my teammates. This guy had just transferred from another school because he'd gotten kicked off his basketball team due to drug usage, and the Florida State Seminoles picked him up.

As we were walking, we were going back and forth. And I could tell something was heavy on his heart and life. He just looked at me and here's what he said. "Ed, there's something different about you, man." He said, "I want what you have."

I was ambushed by the power of God in that moment. I knew God was cracking open the door for me to walk through. So I began to talk to this guy about my life. I simply told him about what had happened to me and how I had come to know Jesus. And God began to take over the conversation. About five hours later I found myself in my friend's dorm room leading him in a prayer to commit his life to Christ. With tears streaming down his cheeks, I saw this guy step over the line of faith and become a believer.

In the Bible, Jesus said,

Ask and it will be given to you; seek and you will find; knock and the door will be opened to you.
—Matthew 7:7

We need people in our lives that pray for and

with us. We need those who will knock on the door on our behalf. And we ourselves need to remember the power of prayer as we pray for others. We need those who will pray those high-risk prayers. How do you PRAY? You talk to God. Break it down this way:

- Start by **P**raising Him for who he is and what he has done.
- Next, **R**epent, which simply means admitting your shortcomings and committing to doing a complete 180.
- Then, **A**sk God for whatever it is you want to ask of Him.
- Finally, **Y**ield to his plan and purpose.

Prayer is not just about getting what we want. Prayer is getting to a point where we want what God wants.

You want to know who the right "they" are? They are the ones who will pray for what God wants. They are the ones who will pray to help you stay above the fray so you won't become prey for the enemy!

SHADE FORTY-NINE: T.L.C.

The enemy, Satan, is all about getting you and me off of God's purpose for our lives. He does everything he can to destroy our lives. You can't look at the amount of relational wreckage in our world and tell me there is not an evil force at work wreaking havoc on our relationships.

The right "they," though, make the devil nervous. When their feet hit the floor in the morning, the devil says, "Oh crap, they're awake!" They are a threat to the enemy's schemes. And since he has no power over us, once we step over the line of faith in Christ, he tries everything he can to trip us up by his version of T.L.C.

- T = Temptation. Temptation is like a painting contest. While God is working on his masterpiece in our lives, the enemy (the tempter) paints his version—a counterfeit. The devil might be painting a picture of lust or toxic anger or insecurity. While he is doing that, the Holy Spirit is painting a picture of integrity, holiness, or potential. The question is, which one are you supplying with the art supplies of your life?

- L = Lies. The devil speaks only one language: lie-ese. He tries to tell us, "There's nothing wrong with just one glance at my painting." And if we take one glance, he tries to get us to take another. And eventually, he whispers to us, "Go ahead and give me the art supplies. You can just help me with this. It will be fun."

- C = Condemnation. Once we fall for the enemy's schemes and trip up, he is in our ear, constantly condemning us. "You messed up again! You can never be a good spouse again, a good friend again. God can never use you again." And he tries his best to convince us that we are useless to God.

Whenever you are feeling this kind of T.L.C., recognize that it is from the enemy. God, on the other hand, has the true sense of TLC: tender loving care.

The right "they" understand God's TLC.

In fact, that's been God's M.O. from the very beginning of time. The first reference to God's character in the Bible is one of compassion. After Adam and Eve were tempted, bought the lie from Satan, and were condemned by him, God stepped in and had compassion on them. God understands that we're going to slip up. We aren't perfect. But he has done the work to cover us. He has felt our pain and wants us to understand that:

> *There is therefore now no condemnation for those who are in Christ Jesus....*
> —Romans 8:1 (nkjv)

SHADE FIFTY:
MASTERPIECE

I began this book with a question: Do you have the right "they" in your life?

Hopefully, as you have read through the previous forty-nine shades you've been able to properly answer that question. But for this last shade, I wrap it up with the final and most important one of all—the shade that changes everything. All the other stuff in the book is great. But it's all secondary compared to this primary color.

God, who created everything, created your life to be a masterpiece. The problem is, just like the first man and woman, Adam and Eve, we take the art supplies out of God's hands and put them into our own. We choose to go our own way, do our own thing, and with one stroke of the brush we turn God's masterpiece into a disasterpiece.

God could have taken his work of art (us) and tossed it in the trash, but he didn't. Instead, he began his greatest work of art yet, his ultimate masterpiece. God sent his only Son, Jesus, into the world to give his life for us. And now, if we choose to receive his free gift and hand over the art supplies of our lives to him, he can wipe our slates clean like a fresh canvas and begin a new work of art, turning a disasterpeice into a masterpiece.

So I leave you with one final question: have you handed over the art supplies of your life to Jesus so he can begin painting in your life? Because HE is the ultimate THEY. And **THEY** are everything.

ACKNOWLEDGEMENTS

When someone sets out to write a book, they begin a journey that can only be completed with the support, assistance, and direction of a great group of people. As this book talks about, the right "they" are crucial in every area of life – including the writing of a book. I want to recognize some people who helped this book become what it is.

First of all, to Lisa, thank you for your unwavering support and creative help every step of the way. I continue to experience the realities that are captured in this book, because you have been my right "they" for more than thirty-nine years!

I would also like to thank some of the amazing team at Fellowship Church. To Andy Boyd, Derric Bonnot, LeeBeth Young, and Calen Chrestman – thank you for your dedication and drive in composing, developing, writing, and editing these pages. Your work helped my words from the stage at Fellowship Church come to life on paper.

To Esther Fedorkevich and the amazing team at The Fedd Agency, thank you for your expertise and direction in making this book a reality.

Finally, to the people of Fellowship Church, thank you for the honor of being your pastor for the past twenty-five years. The truths and insights shared in this book are the result of the time we have spent growing together.

ABOUT
ED YOUNG

Ed Young is the senior pastor of Fellowship Church, one of North America's most attended churches over the past decade. Creative, compelling, and challenging, Ed is known for his bold approach to leadership, unmatched creativity, and ability to make the complex simple, Ed helps people everywhere understand their purpose and their potential from God's perspective.

In addition to being a senior pastor at Fellowship Church, Ed Young is also a *New York Times* best-selling author. He has written several books on leadership and relationships including: *Sexperiment* (Faith Words – 2012); *The Marriage Mirror; Outrageous, Contagious Joy* (Penguin); *The Creative Leader* (Broadman & Holman); *The Creative Marriage* and *Kid CEO* (Warner Faith).

Ed Young has been married to his wife Lisa for over 30 years. The couple has four children and resides in the Dallas/Fort Worth area.